Traditional
ENGLISH COOKING

by Janice Murfitt
Illustrated by Jo Canessa

First published in Great Britain in 1994 by
Parragon Book Service Ltd
Unit 13–17
Avonbridge Trading Estate
Atlantic Road
Avonmouth
Bristol BS11 9QD

A CIP catalogue record for this book is available from the British Library.

ISBN 1 85813 609 1

Edited, designed and typeset by Haldane Mason, London
Editor: Joanna Swinnerton

Printed in Italy

Note: Cup measurements in this book are for American cups. Tablespoons are assumed to be 15ml. Unless otherwise stated, milk is assumed to be full-fat, eggs are standard size 2 and pepper is freshly ground black pepper.

CONTENTS

KEDGEREE

This Indian dish was brought back to England in Victorian times and was adopted by the British. It consisted of rice, lentils, hot spices, eggs and onions.

SERVES ❹

250 g/8 oz/generous cup long-grain rice

500 g/1 lb smoked haddock fillet

60 g/2 oz/¼ cup butter

1 large onion, chopped finely

1 tbsp Madras curry paste

4 tbsp double (heavy) cream

salt and pepper

TO GARNISH

4 hard-boiled (hard-cooked) eggs, shelled

2 tbsp chopped parsley

1 Cook the rice in plenty of boiling salted water for 8–10 minutes until almost tender. Drain in a sieve (strainer) and rinse with hot water.

2 Cook the haddock in 2.5 cm/1 inch of simmering water in a saucepan until it is just tender. Remove with a perforated spoon and set aside to cool. Remove the skin from the fish and flake into pieces using a fork.

3 Cut the hard-boiled (hard-cooked) eggs in half and remove the yolks. Rub the yolks and whites through a sieve (strainer) into separate bowls.

4 Melt the butter in a saucepan, add the onion and curry paste and cook for 2–3 minutes until tender. Stir in the rice and pepper.

5 Heat the rice, stirring occasionally, until it is hot, then add the fish and cream. Turn the mixture gently to heat through.

4

6 Transfer the mixture to a warmed serving dish and garnish the kedgeree with alternate lines of sieved egg yolk, egg white and parsley.

Traditionally, the garnish was arranged in the shape of St Andrew's Cross.

SCRAMBLED EGGS AND SMOKED SALMON

SERVES 4

6 large eggs (size 1)

3 tbsp single (light) cream

125 g/4 oz smoked salmon

30 g/1 oz/2 tbsp butter

4 large slices buttered toast

pepper

Scrambled or rumbled eggs have been a popular breakfast dish in England since Victorian times. Served with smoked salmon, crispy bacon, mushrooms or tomatoes, this makes a nutritious breakfast dish.

1 Put the eggs and cream into a bowl and beat until just blended. Cut the smoked salmon into bite-sized pieces.

2 Put the butter and some pepper into a saucepan. Melt the butter, add the eggs, stirring constantly, and lower the heat.

3 Cook gently until the eggs are soft and creamy. Quickly stir in the smoked salmon, then scoop the eggs out of the pan immediately to prevent further cooking. Serve on slices of hot buttered toast.

CUMBERLAND BRUNCH

SERVES ❹

60 g/2 oz/¼ cup butter

4 lamb's kidneys, skinned, cored and sliced

125 g/4 oz/1 cup button mushrooms

4 tomatoes, halved

500 g/1 lb Cumberland sausage

4 eggs

salt and pepper

6 slices hot buttered toast to serve

Cumberland sausages are instantly recognizable by their shape, as they are very long and are wound into neat coils. If unavailable, use any high quality sausage flavoured with herbs and spices.

1 Melt the butter in a grill (broiler) pan under a preheated moderately hot grill (broiler).

2 Turn the kidneys, mushrooms and tomatoes in the melted butter in the grill (broiler) pan to coat evenly. Sprinkle with some salt and pepper.

3 Brush the sausage with a little melted butter and place on the rack in the grill (broiler) pan over the kidneys, mushrooms and tomatoes. Cook under the grill (broiler) for 5–8 minutes on each side, turning only once, until golden brown.

4 Remove the sausage from the grill (broiler), place on a serving dish and keep warm.

5 Replace the grill (broiler) pan and cook the tomatoes, kidneys and mushrooms

until tender. Remove with a perforated spoon and place on the serving dish with the sausage.

6 Break each egg into the grill (broiler) pan and cook for 2–3 minutes until set. Lift out carefully using a fish slice and arrange on the serving dish. Serve immediately with hot buttered toast.

DEVILLED KIDNEYS

SERVES 4

8 whole lamb's kidneys

30 g/1 oz/2 tbsp butter

MARINADE

2 tsp mustard powder

2 tsp wholegrain mustard

1 tbsp mango chutney

1 tbsp Worcestershire sauce

2 tsp lemon juice

¼ tsp chilli powder

½ tsp salt

TO GARNISH

chopped parsley

lemon wedges

triangles of toast

'Devilled' means cooking with hot condiments, and was once a way of masking slightly 'off' food before the days of refrigeration. These days it is simply a delicious way of tenderizing and flavouring meat before cooking.

1 Using a sharp knife, cut each kidney in half. Remove the skin and core.

2 Put all the ingredients for the marinade in a shallow dish and mix together well. Turn the kidneys in the mixture to coat evenly, cover and leave in a cool place for at least 1 hour.

3 Melt the butter in a frying pan (skillet) or flameproof dish. Lift the kidneys out of the marinade using a perforated spoon and fry quickly on both sides to brown evenly.

4 Add the marinade and cook gently for about 3 minutes until the kidneys are tender. Sprinkle with chopped parsley and garnish with wedges of lemon and triangles of toast.

Devilled Kidneys

MINER'S PASTY

The 'foot', as this dish was once known, was named because of its shape. It fitted neatly into the miners' oval tins, designed to suit the cramped conditions in the mines. Sometimes the 'heel' was filled with a fruit filling and the 'sole' with meat or cheese.

SERVES ❷

300 g/10 oz/2½ cups plain (all-purpose) flour

½ tsp salt

60 g/2 oz/¼ cup white vegetable fat (shortening)

90 g/3 oz/⅓ cup butter

beaten egg to glaze

FILLING

1 small onion, sliced thinly

60 g/2 oz Cheddar cheese, sliced thinly

2 rashers (slices) streaky (fatty) bacon, chopped

1 small apple, sliced thinly

½ tsp mustard powder

2 tbsp ale (light beer)

salt and pepper

1 Sift the flour and salt into a large mixing bowl. Cut the fat and butter into pieces, add to the flour and rub in with your fingertips until the mixture resembles fine breadcrumbs.

2 Stir in 2–3 tbsp cold water and mix with a fork to form a firm dough. Knead lightly on a lightly floured work surface (counter). Roll out half the pastry into an oval shape about 25 x 20 cm/10 x 8 inches, and trim to neaten. Then roll one end of the pastry even thinner, just to the centre, until it is roughly pear-shaped. Cut in half down the centre to give two 'foot' shapes, separate the two halves and place apart on a lightly floured baking sheet.

3 Arrange the onion, cheese, bacon and apple on the feet in layers, seasoning each layer with mustard, salt and pepper. Leave a 1 cm/½ inch space around the edge. Spoon the ale (light beer) over each foot to moisten.

4 Roll out the remaining pastry dough in the same way but 2.5 cm/1 inch larger all round, and cut into two feet as before. Brush the edges of each piece with beaten egg, place each larger shape over its matching half, seal well and mark all around with a fork. Brush with beaten egg, place in a preheated oven at 220°C, 425°F, Gas Mark 7 and bake for 25–30 minutes, or until the feet are golden brown. Serve hot or cold.

PAN HAGGERTY

SERVES 4

60 g/2 oz/¼ cup butter

750 g/1½ lb potatoes, sliced thinly

250 g/8 oz onions, thinly sliced

175 g/6 oz/1½ cups Lancashire (New York State white) cheese, grated

1 tsp mustard powder

salt and pepper

This tasty dish comes from the north of England and is made with layers of potatoes, onion and cheese. Lancashire cheese, pale and mildly flavoured, is often referred to as 'toaster' because it melts so well.

1 Melt the butter in a frying pan (skillet). Arrange a layer of potato slices and onion rings over the base of the pan.

2 Sprinkle with some of the grated cheese, some of the mustard powder, and salt and pepper. Continue to layer the ingredients in the pan, finishing with a layer of grated cheese.

3 Cover the pan with a lid or foil and cook over a gentle heat for about 30 minutes or until the potatoes are tender.

4 Remove the lid or foil from the pan and place under a preheated grill (broiler) until the surface of the Pan Haggerty is golden brown and bubbling. Serve immediately.

PARSNIP CAKES

An old English vegetable, parsnips were known as 'parsneps'; 'neps' meant roots, hence 'turneps' and 'parsneps'. The potato came into favour simply because the texture and flavour was similar to that of parsnips – the first potato was the sweet potato.

SERVES ❹

500 g/1 lb parsnips, chopped

15 g/½ oz/1 tbsp butter

30 g/1 oz/¼ cup plain (all-purpose) flour

¼ tsp ground mace

1 tbsp chopped fresh chives

2 eggs, beaten

125 g/4 oz/2 cups fresh white breadcrumbs

oil for frying

salt and pepper

parsley sprigs to garnish

1 Cook the parsnips in boiling salted water until tender. Drain and mash thoroughly.

2 Beat in the butter, flour, mace, salt, pepper and chives. Spread the mixture over a plate to a depth of 2.5 cm/1 inch, cover and leave until cold.

3 Cut the mixture into 8 equal portions and mould into flat, round shapes.

4 Put the beaten eggs in a dish and the breadcrumbs on a plate, coat each parsnip cake twice in egg and breadcrumbs.

5 Heat about 1 cm/½ inch oil in a frying pan (skillet) until hot, add 4 parsnip cakes at a time and fry on each side for 2–3 minutes until golden brown, turning only once.

6 Drain on paper towels and keep warm. Repeat to fry the remaining parsnip cakes and arrange on a warmed serving dish garnished with sprigs of parsley.

PEASE PUDDING

SERVES ❻

500 g/1 lb/2 cups dry green split peas, soaked overnight

600 ml/1 pint/2½ cups water

2 tbsp chopped fresh mint

1 tsp sugar

60 g/2 oz/¼ cup butter

salt and pepper

Pease pudding is one of the oldest English dishes. After the peas were soaked, they were hung up in a cloth to swell and then cooked with simmering pork or bacon. Serve with bacon or boiled beef.

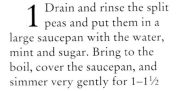

1 Drain and rinse the split peas and put them in a large saucepan with the water, mint and sugar. Bring to the boil, cover the saucepan, and simmer very gently for 1–1½ hours or until the peas are tender. Drain well.

2 Rub the peas through a sieve (strainer) or work in a food processor until smooth. Add the butter with some salt and pepper and blend evenly.

3 Transfer the mixture to a warmed dish and serve immediately.

STUFFED MARROW

The marrow (summer squash) came to England towards the end of the nineteenth century. Young marrows had their centres removed and were steamed upright either with a hot filling, or were filled when cold with a vegetable mayonnaise mixture.

SERVES 4

60 g/2 oz/¼ cup butter, melted

1 small young marrow (summer squash)

2 tomatoes, peeled and chopped

60 g/2 oz/½ cup button mushrooms, chopped finely

60 g/2 oz/1 cup fresh brown breadcrumbs

1 tbsp chopped parsley

1 tbsp chopped fresh sage

1 egg, beaten

salt and pepper

1 Lightly butter a shallow ovenproof dish.

2 Peel the marrow (summer squash), cut a slice off the end and reserve. Discard the seeds.

3 Mix together in a bowl the tomatoes, mushrooms, breadcrumbs, parsley, sage, salt and pepper until well blended. Add just enough beaten egg to bind the filling together; the marrow (summer squash) is full of water and will make the filling moist. Spoon the filling into the cavity of the marrow (summer squash). Replace the end slice and secure with cocktail sticks (toothpicks).

4 Place the marrow (summer squash) in the buttered dish and brush with the remaining melted butter. Place in a preheated oven at 190°C, 375°F, Gas Mark 5, and bake for 30–40 minutes until tender.

5 Tilt up the open end of the stuffed marrow (summer

20

squash) on a wedge of bread to retain the filling when the cocktail sticks (toothpicks) are discarded. Serve immediately.

LETTUCE SOUP

SERVES 6

30 g/1 oz/2 tbsp butter

60 g/2 oz/½ cup onion, chopped

2 round (Boston) lettuce, shredded

1 tbsp plain (all-purpose) flour

600 ml/1 pint/¼ cup vegetable stock

300 ml/½ pint/1¼ cups milk

2 egg yolks

4 tbsp single (light) cream

single (light) cream to serve

salt and pepper

TO GARNISH

chopped fresh chervil and mint

fried or toasted croûtons

Lettuce was eaten in England as far back as the fifteenth century, and was grown in almost every cottage garden. As well as having many culinary uses, lettuces were one of the earliest drugs, as the juice from the stems was thought to be soporific.

1 Melt the butter in a saucepan, add the onion and cook gently, stirring occasionally, until the onion is tender.

2 Add the lettuce and cook for a further 2 minutes, stirring occasionally. Remove the pan from the heat.

3 Stir in the flour, vegetable stock, milk, salt and pepper, return to the heat and bring to the boil. Cover the saucepan and

cook gently for 5 minutes.

4 Rub the soup through a sieve (strainer) or put into a food processor and work until smooth.

5 Return the soup to a clean saucepan and bring to the boil. Blend together the egg yolks and cream, stir into the boiling soup and remove from the heat.

6 Serve the soup hot or cold, garnished with chervil, mint and croûtons. Add an extra spoonful of cream to each serving if desired.

TROUT WITH WATERCRESS SAUCE

SERVES ❹

4 freshwater trout, cleaned

2 tbsp plain (all-purpose) flour

3 tbsp milk

60 g/2 oz/¼ cup butter, melted

salt and pepper

SAUCE

1 bunch watercress, stalks removed

15 g/½ oz/1 tbsp butter

15 g/½ oz/2 tbsp plain (all-purpose) flour

300 ml/½ pint/1¼ cups milk

¼ tsp freshly grated nutmeg

1 tsp lemon juice

2 tbsp double (heavy) cream

TO GARNISH

lemon wedges

watercress sprigs

Freshwater trout was once widely available in England, and people followed special trout streams for miles to fish the trout. Likewise, watercress grew wild in most streams, and could be freshly gathered in abundance.

1 Wash and dry the trout on paper towels. Mix together the flour and some salt and pepper on a plate. Pour the milk into a shallow dish. Dip each trout into the milk and coat evenly with the flour mixture, then place on a platter and keep cool until required.

2 To make the sauce, plunge the watercress leaves into boiling water, then drain thoroughly and chop finely. Put the butter, flour and milk into a saucepan with some salt and pepper. Whisk together over a moderate heat until the sauce boils and thickens. Cook for 2 minutes. Remove the sauce from the heat.

3 Brush the trout with half of the melted butter. Place under a preheated hot grill (broiler) and cook for 3–4 minutes until lightly browned. Turn the trout over, brush the surface with the remaining melted

butter and place under the grill (broiler) again for 3–4 minutes until tender.

4 Reheat the sauce, stir in the watercress, nutmeg, lemon juice and cream and pour into a warmed sauce boat. Arrange the trout on a warmed serving dish and garnish with lemon wedges and fresh watercress sprigs.

SOLE FILLETS IN POTATO JACKETS

SERVES 4

4 large oval-shaped baking potatoes

60 g/2 oz/¼ cup butter, softened

1 tbsp chopped fresh chives

1 tbsp chopped parsley

1 tsp finely grated lemon rind

1 small sole, filleted

1 egg yolk

3 tbsp double (heavy) cream

½ tsp freshly grated nutmeg

90 g/3 oz/½ cup peeled prawns (shrimp)

salt and pepper

TO GARNISH

sprigs of watercress

whole prawns (shrimp)

This recipe was originally called 'Soles (Souls) in Coffins'. 'Coffyn' is a medieval pie crust raised or moulded to give a box-shaped pastry case. This is a quick version using fillets of sole and jacket potatoes.

1 Scrub the potatoes and pierce the skins with a pointed knife. Place on a baking sheet in a preheated oven at 200°C, 400°F, Gas Mark 6, and bake for 1¼ hours or until tender.

2 Put the butter, chives, parsley, lemon rind, salt and pepper into a bowl and beat together until well blended.

3 Cut each fish fillet in half down the length and spread a quarter of the herb butter over each. Roll up neatly, cover and chill.

4 Slice the top off each cooked potato and reserve these as lids. Scoop out the remaining potato into a bowl, keeping the 'coffins' intact.

5 Mash the potato until free from lumps. Beat in the egg yolk, cream, nutmeg, salt and pepper until the potato is smooth and creamy.

26

6 Spread a layer of potato over the base of each 'coffin', and fit the rolled sole fillets neatly inside. Sprinkle each with a few prawns (shrimp) and top with enough potato to fill the 'coffin'.

7 Replace the lids and return the potatoes to the oven for 20 minutes. Serve garnished with watercress and whole prawns (shrimp).

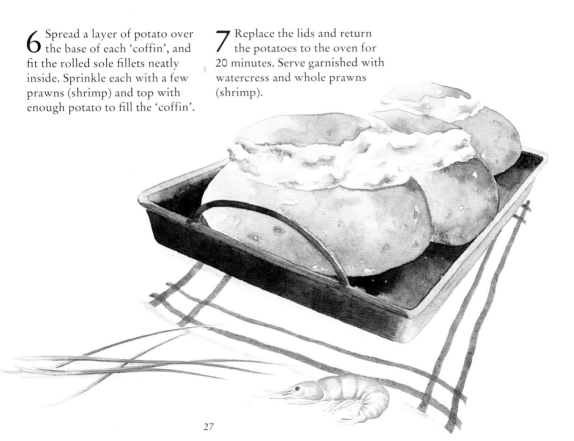

FISH PIE

SERVES ❹

300 ml/½ pint/1¼ cups milk

1 onion, quartered

1 bay leaf

10 fresh mussels

750 g/1½ lb potatoes

3 tbsp single (light) cream

175 g/6 oz smoked haddock

175 g/6 oz cod fillet

30 g/1 oz/¼ cup plain (all-purpose) flour

30 g/1 oz/¼ cup butter

1 tbsp chopped parsley

1 tbsp chopped fresh chervil

175 g/6 oz/1 cup prawns (shrimp), peeled

2 eggs, hard-boiled (hard-cooked)

2 tomatoes

salt and pepper

For people who lived on the coast, fish was always plentiful and fresh. When the trawlers or fishing boats came in, assorted fish was sold cheaply. Fish pie was a popular way of making a tasty dish with a mixture of fish and shellfish.

1 Lightly butter an ovenproof dish. Remove the beards from the mussels and scrub the shells.

2 Put the milk, onion, bay leaf, salt and pepper into a saucepan. Bring to the boil, then remove from the heat. Add the mussels, cover the pan with a lid and leave until the shells have opened. Remove the mussels with a perforated spoon. Cover the milk and leave until cold.

3 Cook the potatoes in boiling salted water until tender. Drain and mash thoroughly. Add the cream and some pepper and beat until smooth and creamy. Place in a nylon piping bag fitted with a medium-sized nozzle (tip).

4 Cut the smoked haddock and cod fillet into thin strips. Remove the mussels from their shells, discarding any that remain closed. Strain the milk and rinse the pan. Put the flour, butter and milk in the clean pan and place over a moderate heat, whisking constantly.

5 Bring to the boil and cook gently for 2 minutes, then remove from the heat. Stir in the parsley, chervil, strips of fish,

mussels and prawns (shrimp) until evenly blended.

6 Place half the mixture into the prepared dish. Peel and quarter the tomatoes and the eggs and scatter them over the fish. Cover with the remaining mixture.

7 Pipe the potato over the top to cover the surface. Place in a preheated oven at 190°C, 375°F, Gas Mark 5 and bake for about 20 minutes until golden brown and bubbling. Serve hot.

STARGAZY PIE

This eighteenth-century recipe originated in Cornwall. The fish were arranged on a pastry-lined plate with their heads on the rim of the pastry. It was wasteful to cover the inedible part of the fish with pastry, so they were left exposed to 'gaze at the stars'.

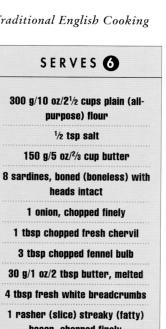

SERVES 6

300 g/10 oz/2½ cups plain (all-purpose) flour

½ tsp salt

150 g/5 oz/⅔ cup butter

8 sardines, boned (boneless) with heads intact

1 onion, chopped finely

1 tbsp chopped fresh chervil

3 tbsp chopped fennel bulb

30 g/1 oz/2 tbsp butter, melted

4 tbsp fresh white breadcrumbs

1 rasher (slice) streaky (fatty) bacon, chopped finely

1 egg

180 ml/6 fl oz/¾ cup milk

saffron strands

salt and pepper

1 Lightly flour a 25 cm/10 inch round pie plate.

2 To make the pastry dough, sift the flour and salt into a large mixing bowl. Cut the butter into pieces and rub into the flour with your fingertips until it resembles fine breadcrumbs. Add 3–4 tbsp cold water and mix with a fork to form a firm dough. Knead on a lightly floured work surface (counter) until smooth.

3 Roll out half the pastry dough and use it line the floured pie plate. Trim off the excess dough.

4 Wash the fish and dry on paper towels. Mix the onion, chervil, fennel, salt and pepper with the melted butter and use to fill the cavity of each fish.

5 Arrange the sardines radiating out from the centre of the dish, their heads on the rim of the pastry dough and their tails overlapping in the centre. Sprinkle with the breadcrumbs and bacon.

6 Beat the egg and 150 ml/ ¼ pint/⅔ cup of the milk together, add some salt and pepper and pour over the fish. Mix the remaining milk and

saffron strands together and use to brush the edge of the pastry dough in between the heads of the sardines.

7 Roll out the remaining dough into a circle large enough to cover the sardines, leaving their heads exposed. Press the pastry together in between the heads. Brush the top of the pie with the saffron milk, place in a preheated oven at 190°C, 375°F, Gas Mark 5, and bake for 45–50 minutes until

the pastry is lightly browned. Garnish the edge of the pie with fresh herbs if liked. Cut into slices between the fish to serve.

WHITEBAIT

These tiny silvery fish are at their best in spring and summer, and are very simple to cook, as they are too small to need gutting or topping and tailing. This recipe is the most common way of preparing them.

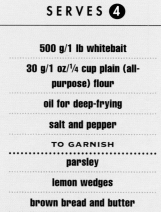

1 Rinse the whitebait in fresh salted water and drain well on paper towels.

2 Sift the flour and sprinkle with the black pepper over a tea-towel (dish cloth) or piece of muslin (cheesecloth).

3 Turn the whitebait in the flour, tossing and shaking the cloth to coat the fish lightly but evenly, taking care not to break any of them.

4 Heat the oil in a deep-fat pan (kettle) until hot (190°C, 370°F). Place one third of the whitebait in the frying basket, plunge it quickly into the hot oil and then lift it out almost immediately.

5 Drain on paper towels. Fry the remaining whitebait in the same way. Serve piled high on a warm serving platter and garnished with parsley, lemon wedges and brown bread and butter.

Whitebait

HONEY-GLAZED YORK HAM

The original York hams were renowned for their flavour, which was obtained from the burning of the oak sawdust from the building of one of England's great cathedrals, York Minster.

SERVES 8

- 2 kg/4 lb knuckle end of gammon (ham), soaked overnight
- 2 carrots, sliced thickly
- 2 celery sticks, sliced thickly
- 1 turnip, chopped roughly
- 2 onions, quartered
- 1 tsp black peppercorns
- 2 bay leaves
- sprigs parsley and fresh thyme
- 2 tbsp clear honey
- grated rind and juice of 2 oranges
- 1 tbsp whole cloves
- 1 tbsp demerara sugar (sugar crystals)
- orange wedges to garnish

1 Place the gammon (ham) in a large saucepan and cover with fresh cold water. Bring to the boil, discard the water and remove the gammon.

2 Arrange the prepared vegetables over the base of the saucepan. Place the gammon (ham) on the bed of vegetables with the peppercorns, bay leaves, parsley and thyme. Cover with cold water and bring to the boil slowly. Skim the surface with a perforated spoon, cover and simmer very gently for 45 minutes.

3 Cool the gammon (ham) in the water, then remove. Peel off the skin and score the surface with a sharp knife to make a diamond pattern. Place in a roasting tin (pan).

4 Mix together the honey, orange rind and juice in a bowl. Brush the surface of the gammon (ham) with one third of the mixture and stud the surface with cloves.

5 Place in a preheated oven at 200°C, 400°F, Gas Mark 6,

34

and bake for 40 minutes, spooning over half of the remaining glaze during this time.

6 Remove the gammon (ham) from the oven, spoon over the remaining glaze and sprinkle with demerara sugar (sugar crystals). Return to the oven for a further 10–15 minutes.

7 Place the gammon (ham) on a ham stand or board to carve. Use the juices in the roasting tin (pan) to make gravy if wished. Serve hot or cold, garnished with orange wedges.

35

YORKSHIRE PUDDING

Yorkshire pudding is often served with onion gravy as a starter. This tradition dates back to when meat was a luxury, especially for poorer people, so eating Yorkshire pudding first blunted the appetite, and only small portions of meat were needed to follow.

SERVES ❹

15 ml (1 tbsp) oil or white fat

115 g (4 oz) plain flour

2.5 ml (½ tsp) salt

1 tbsp oil or white vegetable fat (shortening)

125 g/4 oz/1 cup plain (all-purpose) flour

½ tsp salt

2 eggs, beaten

150 ml/¼ pint/⅔ cup milk

150 ml/¼ pint/⅔ cup water

pepper

1 Put a little oil or white vegetable fat (shortening) in 2 trays of 8 individual Yorkshire pudding tins (muffin pans), or one large baking tin (pan).

2 Sift the flour, salt and pepper into a mixing bowl. Make a well in the centre and add the beaten egg and milk. Mix together with a wooden spoon and beat until smooth. Beat in the water gradually to make a smooth batter. Cover and leave in a cool place until ready to cook.

3 Place the tins in a preheated oven at 220°C, 425°F, Gas Mark 7 for 5 minutes or until the oil or fat is very hot. Divide the mixture between the tins (pans) and return quickly to the oven for 25–30 minutes until well risen, golden brown and firm.

Serve with gravy as a starter to precede any roast meat, or serve as an accompaniment to roast beef.

ROAST BEEF

3 kg/6 lb forerib of beef (prime rib roast), chined

The roast beef of Old England is world-famous and is still today perhaps the most cherished national dish. Large joints of beef were cooked on a spit over an open fire and the Yorkshire pudding was cooked in the tin underneath the beef in the juices.

1 Stand the beef in a roasting tin (pan) with the fat side uppermost. Place in a preheated oven at 225°C, 425°F, Gas Mark 7. Roast the beef for 30 minutes.

2 Reduce the temperature to 190°C, 375°F, Gas Mark 5 and roast the beef for another 1½ hours, or until cooked to your taste. To estimate the cooking time, allow 20 minutes per 500 g/1 lb for rare beef, 25–30 minutes for medium beef, and 30–35 minutes for well-done beef.

3 Transfer the cooked meat to a warmed serving dish and leave for 15 minutes before carving. During this time the oven temperature may be increased to cook some Yorkshire pudding (see page 36).

4 Serve the meat juices as gravy. This is traditional, but, if you prefer, you could thicken them with a little plain (all-purpose) flour, add some vegetable stock and boil until it has the consistency you want. Serve the beef, carved into slices, with Yorkshire pudding, roast potatoes and vegetables, accompanied by English mustard and horseradish sauce.

Roast Beef

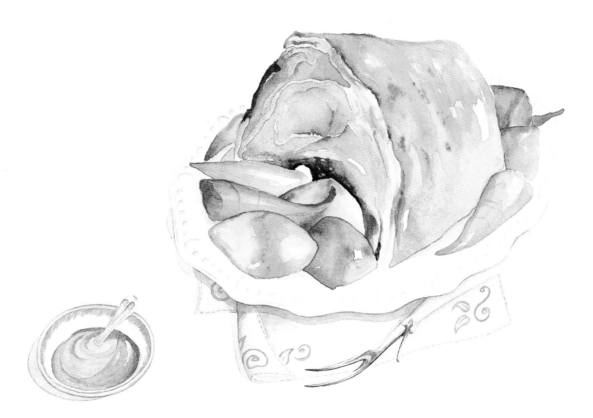

39

ROAST PHEASANT

The shooting season is an English tradition and is limited to certain times of the year. Pheasant should be well hung before eating, to develop the flavour and texture of the meat.

1 Wipe the inside of the pheasant with paper towels and brush with a little of the melted butter. Season the cavity with salt and pepper and put the minced (ground) beef and apple quarters inside. These help to keep the pheasant moist while cooking. Truss the pheasant with string so that it keeps a good shape.

2 Brush the skin of the pheasant with a little of the melted butter and coat in the oatmeal. Place in a small roasting tin (pan) and cover the breast with rashers (slices) of bacon.

3 Place in a preheated oven at 200°C, 400°F, Gas Mark 6. Roast the pheasant undisturbed for 20 minutes, then remove the bacon and baste with some of the melted butter. Cook for a further 20 minutes or until the

juices no longer run pink when the pheasant is pierced close to the bone.

4 Meanwhile heat the remaining melted butter until bubbling and fry the breadcrumbs until golden brown. Transfer to a warmed serving dish.

5 Place the pheasant on a serving platter and allow to stand for 10 minutes before carving. Garnish with sprigs of watercress by the tip of the breast bone, and with the tail feathers. Serve carved into slices with the fried breadcrumbs, gooseberry jelly and game chips.

PORK AND ANCHOVY PIE

This is better known to many as Melton Mowbray Pie, the home of the English pork pie. There are many different pork pie recipes, but it is the anchovy essence that makes the Melton Mowbray Pie special.

SERVES 6

PASTRY (DOUGH)

300 g/10 oz/2½ cups plain (all-purpose) flour

½ tsp salt

1 egg yolk

90 g/3 oz/⅓ cup white fat (shortening)

150 ml/¼ pint/⅔ cup water

beaten egg to glaze

FILLING

750 g/1½ lb boneless pork,

2 tsp anchovy essence (paste)

2 tsp chopped fresh sage

2 tsp chopped fresh marjoram

JELLIED STOCK

300 ml/½ pint/1¼ cups chicken stock

15 g/½ oz/1 envelope powdered gelatine

1 Sift the flour and salt into a bowl. Make a well in the centre and add the egg yolk. Heat the fat (shortening) and water in a saucepan until the fat has melted, then bring rapidly to the boil. Add the boiling liquid immediately to the flour and beat to form a soft dough. Knead lightly until smooth and elastic, then leave in a plastic bag in a warm place for 30 minutes.

2 Grease and lightly flour the outer surface of a pudding basin 10 cm/4 inches in diameter, and cut a double-thickness strip of greaseproof paper (baking parchment) to fit around the outside. Roll out two thirds of the dough to a 20 cm/8 inch round. Invert the dough over the container and mould it firmly and evenly over the base and sides. Trim the edge and fit the paper strip around the outside of the mould. Tie with string and refrigerate until firm.

3 Cut the pork into cubes and mix well with the other filling ingredients and some pepper. Invert the container on to a baking sheet lined with baking parchment and ease away from the dough, twisting gently to loosen. Fill the dough with the pork mixture, packing well down the sides to support the shape of the pie.

4 Roll out the remaining dough to make a lid for the pie. Brush the pie rim with egg glaze, position the lid and seal the edges. Trim off the surplus pastry and paper, cut a cross in the centre of the lid and fold back the points. Decorate the lid with leaves made from any trimmings, and a bud to fit loosely over the central hole. Brush with egg glaze.

5 Bake in a preheated oven at 200°C, 400°F, Gas Mark 6 for 30 minutes, reduce the heat to 170°C, 325°F, Gas Mark 3, cover with greaseproof paper (baking parchment) and cook for a further 1¼ hours. Leave on the baking sheet until cold.

6 Sprinkle the gelatine on to the boiling stock and stir until dissolved. Leave until almost setting, then remove the central bud and pour the stock through the hole in the top of the pie until full. Replace the bud and leave to set in a cool place for 1 hour.

PRUNE-STUFFED CHICKEN WITH LEMON

SERVES ❹

1.5 kg/3 lb oven-ready chicken

1 onion, quartered

1 bay leaf

STUFFING

350 g/12 oz/2 cups prunes, soaked overnight and drained

30 g/1 oz/¼ cup almonds

175 g/6 oz/3 cups fresh white breadcrumbs

1 tbsp each of chopped fresh parsley, rosemary and thyme

30 g/1 oz/3 tbsp suet

2 tbsp malt vinegar

LEMON SAUCE

pared rind and juice of 2 lemons

30 g/1 oz/2 tbsp butter, softened

30 g/1 oz/¼ cup plain (all-purpose) flour

1 tbsp honey

This recipe has survived unchanged for many centuries, and is often known as 'Hindle Wakes' or 'Hen of the Wake'. Wake Night was a vigil held in English villages on the eve of a patron saint's day, and the white meat, dark stuffing, bright lemon sauce and green garnish of this dish graced many a table on this night.

1 To make the stuffing, stone (pit) the prunes and chop finely, chop the almonds and put both in a mixing bowl with the breadcrumbs, herbs, suet, salt and pepper. Add the vinegar and mix together into a firm stuffing.

2 Stuff both ends of the chicken and secure the skin at the neck and tail end with a trussing needle and thin string. Truss into a neat shape using more string.

3 Place the chicken, onion, bay leaf, salt and pepper into a large saucepan or cast-iron casserole and add enough water to reach one third of the height of the chicken. Bring to the boil, cover and simmer very gently for 1 hour. Turn off the heat and allow the chicken to cool in the stock.

4 To make the lemon sauce, put the pared rind and 300 ml/8 fl oz/1 cup water into a saucepan. Bring

to the boil, remove from the heat, cover and allow to cool.

5 Remove the rind and cut into needle-thin shreds and reserve. Blend the butter and flour together to form a paste. Bring the lemon liquor to the boil, whisk in the butter mixture and the lemon juice. Bring to the boil, whisking until thickened, and cook for 2 minutes. Add the lemon shreds and honey, then leave to cool.

6 Drain the chicken well and place on a serving plate. Pour the lemon sauce over to coat evenly. Garnish with halved prunes, lemon wedges and parsley sprigs.

45

CHICKEN AND LEEK PIE

SERVES ❻

1 onion, quartered

1 celery stick, chopped

1 carrot, cut into chunks

1 bay leaf

1.5 kg/3 lb oven-ready chicken

3 leeks, trimmed and sliced

125 g/4 oz ox tongue, sliced

30 g/1 oz/2 tbsp butter

30 g/1 oz/¼ cup plain (all-purpose) flour

1 tbsp chopped parsley

1 tbsp chopped fresh tarragon

250 g/8 oz puff pastry

1 egg, beaten

4 tbsp single (light) cream

salt and pepper

Leeks are always at their best during March and April, and can be used to make flavoursome soups and broths. They were always kept in the garden, even past their season, when they grew quite thick but still had many uses.

1 Put the onion, celery, carrot, bay leaf, salt and pepper in a large saucepan. Place the chicken on top of the vegetables and add enough cold water to cover the chicken.

2 Bring to the boil, cover and simmer gently for 1 hour. Remove the chicken from the stock and set aside to cool.

3 Pour the stock through a sieve (strainer) over a bowl. Return 600 ml/1 pint/2½ cups of the stock to the saucepan, bring to the boil and add the leeks.

4 Cover and cook gently for 3–4 minutes until almost tender. Remove the leeks, reserving the stock, and place in a pie dish.

5 Remove the meat from the chicken, discarding the skin and bones. Cut the chicken into bite-sized pieces and add to the pie dish with the ox tongue.

6 Put the butter and flour in the saucepan, add the reserved stock and whisk together until well blended. Bring to the boil slowly and cook for 1 minute. Add the parsley and tarragon and season

to taste. Pour over the chicken and leeks and leave until cold.

7 Roll out the puff pastry thinly enough to fit the top of the pie dish and to cut off an extra strip of pastry 1 cm/½ inch wide. Cover the rim of the dish with the pastry strip and brush the edges with beaten egg. Top with the pastry lid, seal and flute the edges. Make a hole in the centre.

8 Cut out leaves from the pastry trimmings, arrange on the top of the pie, and brush with beaten egg. Place in a preheated oven at 200°C, 400°F, Gas Mark 6 and bake for 45–50 minutes until golden brown and well risen.

9 Mix the remaining egg and cream together and pour into the pie through the hole in the top. The heat of the pie cooks the egg mixture as soon as it is poured in.

LAMB CUTLETS WITH REDCURRANT AND ROSEMARY

Lamb roasted with fragrant rosemary is a time-honoured combination for a very good reason. This would make a sumptuous dinner party dish or a highly acceptable substitute for the traditional Sunday roast leg of lamb.

SERVES 4

30 g/1 oz/2 tbsp butter

2 sprigs fresh rosemary

4 lamb leg steaks about 2.5 cm/ 1 inch thick

2 tbsp redcurrant jelly

150 ml/¼ pint/⅔ cup vegetable stock

2 tbsp cornflour (cornstarch)

150 ml/¼ pint/⅔ cup red wine

60 g/2 oz/½ cup fresh redcurrants (optional)

salt and pepper

TO GARNISH

sprigs of fresh rosemary

redcurrant strands

1 Melt the butter in a large frying pan (skillet), add the rosemary sprigs and lamb steaks.

2 Sprinkle the steaks with salt and pepper and fry quickly on both sides to seal. Then reduce the heat and cook gently for 10–15 minutes, turning frequently, until tender.

3 Place the steaks on a serving dish and keep warm. Stir the redcurrant jelly into the herb butter and heat gently until melted.

4 Add the stock and bring to the boil. Blend the cornflour (cornstarch) and red wine together, add to the stock mixture and bring to the boil, stirring constantly.

5 Cook for 2 minutes, add the redcurrants, if using, and pour the sauce over the lamb. Garnish with the rosemary sprigs and redcurrant strands.

DEVONSHIRE SQUAB PIE

The old tradition of carrying a decorated ram on a cart through the streets of a Devon town is still celebrated. Spit-roasted during the night, the ram is sliced and sold the following day. The pie originates from these times, and uses neck lamb chops, apples and spices.

SERVES 4

30 g/1 oz/2 tbsp soft brown sugar

½ tsp ground allspice

1 tbsp plain (all-purpose) flour

1 onion, sliced thinly

1 large cooking apple, peeled, cored and sliced

750 g/1½ lb best end neck chops (rib lamb chops), trimmed

150 ml/¼ pint/⅔ cup vegetable stock

salt and pepper

PASTRY

250 g/8 oz/2 cups plain (all-purpose) flour

60 g/2 oz/¼ cup lard (shortening)

60 g/2 oz/¼ cup butter

milk to glaze

1 Mix the sugar, allspice, salt, pepper and flour together in a bowl.

2 Place half the onion and apple slices in a shallow baking dish. Arrange the chops on top and sprinkle with the flour mixture. Top with the remaining onion and apple slices and pour over the stock.

3 To make the pastry, sift the flour and ½ tsp salt into a mixing bowl. Cut the fats into pieces, add to the flour and rub in with your fingertips until the mixture resembles fine breadcrumbs. Stir in about 2 tbsp cold water and mix with a fork to form a firm dough. Knead lightly on a lightly floured work surface (counter).

4 Roll out the dough thinly enough to cover the top of the pie dish and to cut a strip to line the rim of the dish. Moisten the edge of the dish, fit the strip and pie top and seal the edges. Cut

50

up the edge and flute with your fingertips. Garnish the top with leaf shapes cut from the dough trimmings.

5 Brush the pastry dough with milk and place in a preheated oven at 200°C, 400°F, Gas Mark 6. Bake for 35–40 minutes until the pastry is golden

brown and the lamb is tender. Serve hot with assorted vegetables.

BLACKBERRY JUNKET

SERVES 4

250 g/8 oz/1½ cups ripe blackberries

600 ml/1 pint/2½ cups milk

1 tbsp rose water (optional)

30 g/1 oz/2 tbsp caster (superfine) sugar

1 tsp rennet essence (2 unflavoured rennet tablets)

rose petals or extra blackberries to decorate

double (heavy) cream to serve

Junket originated from the west of England. It was made from warm milk straight from the cow and set with rennet, the juices from the lining of a cow's stomach. Rennet is now obtainable commercially, and vegetarian substitutes are available if you prefer.

1 Rub the blackberries through a fine sieve (strainer) using a wooden spoon to extract all the juice. Discard the seeds.

2 Warm the milk until it is just blood heat; do not overheat or the junket will not set. Mix together with the blackberry juice, rose water, if using, and sugar.

3 Pour the blackberry mixture into a serving dish and stir in the rennet essence (follow the package directions if using tablets). Leave to set undisturbed. Do not chill.

4 Decorate the top with a few rose petals or blackberries and leaves. Serve with double (heavy) cream.

Blackberry Junket

BROWN BREAD ICE CREAM

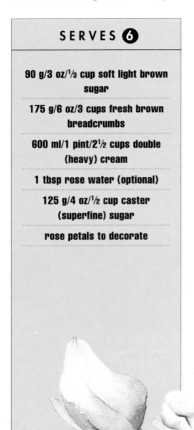

90 g/3 oz/⅓ cup soft light brown sugar

175 g/6 oz/3 cups fresh brown breadcrumbs

600 ml/1 pint/2½ cups double (heavy) cream

1 tbsp rose water (optional)

125 g/4 oz/½ cup caster (superfine) sugar

rose petals to decorate

This recipe dates back to fourteenth-century England and was a delicious way of using up stale bread. The cream was whipped until thick, then coarsely crushed sugar, violet or rose water and 'as much fine breadcrumbs as the cream would carry' were added.

1 Mix together the sugar and breadcrumbs and spread over a baking sheet.

2 Place in a pre-heated oven at 200°C, 400°F, Gas Mark 6 and bake for 10–15 minutes until the sugar has caramelized, stirring occasionally. Leave until cold, then break the mixture into small pieces.

3 Whip the cream until thick. Stir in the rose water, if using, and caster (superfine) sugar and pour into a plastic container. Cover and freeze for 3 hours.

4 Scrape the cream mixture into a bowl and beat until smooth. Add the caramelized breadcrumbs and stir until well blended.

5 Pour back into the plastic container, cover and return to the freezer until firm. Transfer to the refrigerator 30 minutes before serving.

6 Serve in scoops arranged in glass dishes and decorated with rose petals.

SYLLABUB

grated rind of 1 lemon

125 ml/4 fl oz/½ cup lemon juice

125 g/4 oz/½ cup caster (superfine) sugar

175 ml/6 fl oz/¾ cup Madeira wine

2 tbsp brandy

600 ml/1 pint/2½ cups double cream

10 ratafia biscuits (mini macaroons), crumbled

ground cinnamon to dust

Syllabub is also spelt 'Sillebub' and is a mixture of wine and brandy and whipped cream. The name was derived from 'Sill', an area of the Champagne region of France from which the wine 'Sille' took its name. 'Bub' was the common Elizabethan name for a bubbly drink.

1 Place the lemon rind, lemon juice, sugar, Madeira and brandy together in a bowl and whisk until well blended.

2 Pour the cream into the bowl and whip until a fine froth rises to the surface and the mixture has thickened.

3 Divide the crumbled ratafia biscuits (mini macaroons) between 6 serving glasses. Pour an equal amount of the syllabub mixture into each glass and fill to the top.

4 Dust the surface of each syllabub with cinnamon and chill until ready to serve.

FRIAR'S OMELETTE

This early recipe was also called 'Froise Omelette'. 'Froise' crops up in many old cook books, and means 'fried in batter'.

60 g/2 oz/¼ cup butter

500 g/1 lb cooking apples, peeled, cored and sliced

1 tbsp sugar

½ tsp ground mixed spice (apple pie spice)

cider and crushed sugar to serve

BATTER

125 g/4 oz/1 cup plain (all-purpose) flour

2 eggs, separated

300 ml/½ pint/1¼ cups milk

1 Melt the butter in a large frying pan (skillet) until foaming. Add the apple slices and cook in the butter until tender, about 4–5 minutes.

2 Meanwhile, make the batter. Sift the flour into a mixing bowl. Make a well in the centre, add the egg yolks and half of the milk and beat together with a wooden spoon until smooth.

3 Stir in the remaining milk. Whisk the egg whites until stiff and fold into the batter.

4 Remove the apple slices and keep warm.

5 Pour half the batter into the frying pan (skillet). When the surface has set, turn over to brown the other side.

6 Cover the surface with half the apple slices and sprinkle with half the sugar and mixed spice (apple pie spice). Fold over like an omelette and place on a serving dish. Keep warm.

7 Use the remaining
ingredients to make a second
omelette. Place on the serving
dish and pour over a few drops
of cider and sprinkle with sugar.

ENGLISH TRIFLE

Trifle, or 'tipsy cake', was very popular in Victorian England. It was extremely rich and heavily laced with alcohol. Trifle consisted of brandy-soaked sponge fingers, fruit, egg custard and cream and was decorated with almonds and strawberries.

SERVES 8

2 tbsp Madeira wine

1 tbsp brandy

20 sponge fingers (lady-fingers)

2 tbsp strawberry jam (preserves)

250 g/8 oz/1½ cups strawberries, halved

300 ml/½ pint/1¼ cups double (heavy) cream

CUSTARD

2 eggs, plus 2 yolks

30 g/1 oz/2 tbsp caster (superfine) sugar

1 tbsp cornflour (cornstarch)

300 ml/½ pint/1¼ cups milk

1 tsp vanilla flavouring (extract)

TO DECORATE

8 ratafias (mini macaroons) and 8 strawberries and leaves

1 To make the custard, whisk the whole eggs, yolks, sugar and cornflour (cornstarch) together in a bowl until well blended.

2 Place the milk in a saucepan with the vanilla flavouring (extract) and bring to the boil. Pour on to the eggs in the bowl, whisking well.

3 Pour the custard through a sieve (strainer) back into the clean saucepan. Cook over a gentle heat, whisking constantly, until thick. Do not let the custard boil or it will curdle. Leave until cold.

4 Mix together the Madeira and brandy in a shallow dish. Dip one sponge finger (lady-finger) at a time into the brandy mixture, spread with some jam (preserves) and sandwich together with another dipped sponge finger (lady-finger). Place in the base of a glass dish. Repeat with the remaining sponge fingers (lady-fingers), Madeira mixture and jam (preserves) to cover the base of the dish. Pour the remaining Madeira mixture over the sponge fingers (lady-fingers) and cover with two thirds of the

halved strawberries. Whip the cream until it forms peaks.

5 Fold two thirds of the cream into the cold custard until well blended and smooth. Pour over the sponge fingers (lady-fingers) and strawberries in the glass dish.

6 Fill a piping bag, fitted with a small star nozzle (tip), with the remaining cream. Pipe the cream over the top of the custard and decorate with the ratafias (mini macaroons), the remaining strawberries and some strawberry leaves. Chill until required.

61

CABINET PUDDING

SERVES ❹

4 glacé (candied) cherries

8 angelica leaves

125 g/4 oz sponge cake

6 ratafia biscuits (mini macaroons)

2 tbsp toasted flaked (slivered) almonds

4 eggs

600 ml/1 pint/2½ cups milk

60 g/2 oz/¼ cup caster (superfine) sugar

SAUCE

350 g/12 oz/2½ cups raspberries

60 g/2 oz/½ cup icing (confectioners') sugar

In most country households there was always bread flour in the bin, butter in the crock, a cow and hens in the byre, a box of spices in the kitchen and a skillet standing over the fire – all the ingredients needed to make an instant pudding.

1 Grease the sides and line the base of a 15 cm/ 6 inch charlotte mould or soufflé dish with a disc of greaseproof paper (baking parchment). Make a design on the base of the mould using the cherries and angelica leaves.

2 Cut the sponge cake into small pieces and crumble the ratafia biscuits (mini macaroons). Place in a mixing bowl with the almonds.

3 Whisk the eggs well. Put the milk in a saucepan and bring to the boil. Pour on to the beaten egg, whisking well. Stir in the sugar. Strain the custard into the bowl over the sponge cake mixture, stir gently and leave until cold.

4 Tip the cake and custard mixture carefully into the mould and cover with a layer of greaseproof paper (baking parchment) and

foil. Place the mould in a saucepan one quarter filled with simmering water. Cover and cook gently for 1¼ hours or until the pudding feels firm.

5 To make a raspberry sauce, rub the raspberries through a sieve (strainer) and discard the seeds. Stir in the icing

(confectioners') sugar and beat until smooth. Invert the pudding on to a warmed serving dish and pour the sauce around it.

INDEX